Coming Back to Myself

Suzane Andre

BookLeaf Publishing

India | USA | UK

Presentation by *BookLeaf Publishing*

Web: www.bookleafpub.com

E-mail: info@bookleafpub.com

ISBN: 9789363309661

First edition 2024

*This book is dedicated to my children.
Witnessing life through their eyes has
reconnected me with my inner child and gave
me the courage and strength to evolve.*

PREFACE

I never set out to write this book. Initially, many of my poems were laments about the many loves I have experienced and lost over the years. However, along my journey, there were moments of clarity where I paused to assess my life and my connection to the world around me. As I gathered my love poems, I came to a profound realization: the truest love was within me. It became clear that sharing my journey with the world was a far greater gift.

This collection of poems details my spiritual and emotional evolution, pinpointing the significant moments that have shaped me into who I am today. I invite you to join me as I share my reflections from the beginning of my spiritual journey to now.

To feel

A barrier around my heart
A barrier to feel
Have I grieved enough yet
Have I loved myself enough yet
I keep a lot to myself
To protect myself
But I need to break open
To heal

Dolores

The pain
Bubbles up underneath the surface
Like a fountain under pressure
Until it finally explodes
Like a geyser
And no one expects it
And no one can handle it
I stand off to the side
Awkward and alone
Because I don't want to share it
I want to be alone in it
I don't want to be a burden
But it's there
I don't want to be a part of it
But it's there

Amygdala

You get stuck looking for the familiar
The warmth and the promise
That they would be there
And even though they've left
Hell, they might've never been there
You hold onto the familiarity
Their former promises
And you'd rather live in fantasy
Not in this cold, harsh reality
You hold on, hoping
Tomorrow brings a text or a call
Your abandonment wounds triggered
But think of your worth, love
You are not worth what you are offered
Misuse, Abuse, Mistreatment
You are worth far more than that
Beautiful Being
More than a sex toy
More than a warm hearth
More than an amusement
More than a punching bag
You deserve someone as wild about you
As you would be towards them
Real love

The Storm

I've been caught in a storm
For so many years
The land dwellers don't understand
My boat has been battered
And I long to return to shore
With my feet on the ground
No longer tossing in the waves
But the lighthouse is still far off yet
So I captain my boat
With my ever-growing crew
My hands gripped to the wheel
As I keep the boat steady

Stillness

5

I am a leaf
Floating in the wind
Subject to all that life throws at me

I am the eye of the storm
Watching calmly
As the problems whirlwind around me

I am still
But a mess of movement inside
Always watching
Always waiting
Patiently
For my turn to rise

Allowing

I allow myself to be seen
I allow myself to be beautiful
Allowing not masking
Allowing not faking

I allow myself to be heard
I allow myself to be taken seriously
Allowing not asking
Allowing not forcing

I allow myself to be wanted
I allow myself to be loved
Allowing not earning
Allowing not begging

I present myself as myself
Allowing myself to show up
Not worried about judgment
Not letting others' opinion
Be my obstacle
I am worthy
Because I exist

I am learning to love

Destroying as much as I love
Creating
Detaching as much as I love
Attaching
Ending as much as I love
Beginning
Dying as much as I love
Living

Instead of holding onto the positive
I am learning to love
The ebb and the flow

Witness

Witness your own life
You are the witness
While it's nice to have a companion
Anything else is co-dependent
While it's nice to have friends
You don't want to be limited
Live your own life
You are the witness

Truth

I love the taste of truth
Even when it's a bitter pill
I love the smell of truth
Even when it's the stench
Of someone's true nature
I love the touch of truth
Even when I can never
Touch someone ever
I love the sight of truth
I believe my "lying eyes"
Over their lies
I love the sound of truth
It's louder than all the lies
They've ever told me
Truth will always win
Truth never fails
What is done in the dark
Always comes into light

When the lioness awakens

It's when she's the most dangerous
When she refuses to play small
When she refuses to hide in the shadows
When she doesn't accept the status quo
When she challenges when others say no

When she doesn't care about being a bitch
In fact, she's the queen of them
Her moves reflect her royalty
The muttering of peasants means nothing

Because how can someone
Controlled by others
Control her
How can someone not in
Control of themselves
Control her

When her wildness inside awakens
It's when she's the most dangerous

Me time

I made kings
Now it's time to be a queen

I loved him
Now it's time to love me

I gave and I gave
Now I give it all to me

Put up my boundaries
No more codependency

You call me a bitch
But who's fighting for me

You call me selfish
But who's selfless for me

No more holding it down
Watching him shine

It's me time
It's me time
Now it's my time

No one knows

What is in your mind
So why make yourself suffer
In longing or fantasy
Free your mind and reclaim your thoughts
Create the future you want
Alone
And anyone who wants to intersect
Is free to come along for the moment
But this life is yours
Feel into the moment

To be loved

I wanted to be loved
Then I learned
I had to be love
To be my perfect partner
Pour in all the love
And self-care
To emanate beauty
Even when no one was looking
To tell myself
The sweetest words
Even if no one was around
To fully enjoy my company
To experience my life
With me

Instead of waiting
To be loved
I started loving myself
First learning how to love
Then giving it to myself
To love myself as much
As I would want someone else
To love me

Love Letter

The first love letter
I write
Should be to myself
How much I love my body
From my wild hair
All the way down
To my beautiful toes
I love my mind
And the way I'm resourceful
My resilience
I look at how far I've come
And see a hopeful future
Filled with laughter & love
A future of my own creation
Thank you

Mother

15

I had to self-parent
What I didn't learn
To show up for myself
Where I was let down
Little me
Felt like I didn't belong
All along I belonged to me

Breaking the Illusion

I was sold an illusion
Told to stay in line
Check off the boxes
And I would be fine

I was sold an illusion
And when it went wrong
I was told it was all my choice
Told I could never change

I was sold an illusion
And was shamed for rejecting it
Others so happy to pretend
As long as they are placated

I pierced the veil
At first to save my life
Then to better my life
Then to create my life

I was told to get back
Get back into the box
Go back to the normal things
Before I brought about shame

I had no guidance
Stepping into the unknown
Making my own path
As they mocked me behind the veil

But they saw my path
Now they follow my path
Slowly breaking the illusion
Slowly realizing our truth

There is no perfect path
Only our experiences to bear
We are not to judge
Only to love

Recognition

Sometimes I don't recognize myself
But maybe I'm not meant to be
The same
I'm not required to be consistent
Like a character in a book
I'm creation in the flesh
And every morning
I write my story
I put on who needs to experience
This ever-changing day

All I Wanted was the Sound

I'm in need of the healing waters
The healing sound
That drowns out all the noise
Of the world
And allows me to be still
To be fully present
To appreciate
The laughter of a child
The simple joys
We take for granted
But will never experience again
Let me revel in this moment
In its immanence
In its impermanence

Paper Cut Heart

Each heartbreak
Hurts a little less
Just rips a little fabric
Of my torn-apart heart
Teaching me that
I don't have to accept
Just because it's offered
I don't have to stay
Where I'm not appreciated
It's not a failure
Because we are all connected
Under God
It's just not my human
For the rest of my journey

Call of the Void

If I learned anything
I learned
I know nothing

Eventually we all
Get sucked into the void
We complicate our lives
With wars, drama, and lies
To have some semblance of control
In a bid to a-void it

Will they remember me
When it's my turn
Was it worth all this pain
Was my living in vain
I hear it calling my name

If I learned anything
I learned I'm technically nothing
A speck in this universe
But my presence was needed
Contributing to fabric
Of this life we weave

When I go back

I'll give my body back
But my presence I hope
Weaves through this planet
Through the void
And back to the stars

Alchemy

Breathe in the truth
That we are all one being
Fragmented
Our experience
Is our truth
Our connection
Is our light
We come together
Commune
In connection
We breathe
Sharing our truth
We depart
Changed (in alchemy)
We connect
Ever-changing
We leave
Changed (in alchemy)

www.ingramcontent.com/pod-product-compliance
Lightning Source LLC
LaVergne TN
LVHW021357200726